MW01052997

ISBN 0-7683-2115-8

Compiled and Illustrated by
Kathy Davis
© Kathy Davis Designs, 1999
www.kathydavis.com
All rights reserved

Published in 1999 by Cedco Publishing Company
100 Pelican Way, San Rafael, California 94901
For a free catalog of other Cedco® products, please write
to the address above, or visit our website: www.cedco.com

Printed in Hong Kong

1 3 5 7 9 10 8 6 4 2

This book is dedicated with love
to my parents,
Ruth and Frank Consaley,
who have taught me how to appreciate
life's greatest gifts.

A BOOK OF INSPIRATIONS

compiled and illustrated by

Kathy Davis

Cedco Publishing Company . San Rafael, California

A note from the Artist

It is my pleasure to share with you this collection of art and verse celebrating life's precious moments. Assembled in this book are the thoughts of many brilliant authors and philosophers whose messages are timeless. I would like to acknowledge their contributions and thank them for the inspiration their words have given me. My artwork and writing is in response to these great thinkers, as well as to nature and the beauty that surrounds us. My words and images are my "song," which I am honored to share with you. It is my hope that through this song you receive some inspiration to make the moments in your life a beautiful lasting melody. I can think of no greater gift I'd rather give.

Thanks to Peter, Jen, Steve, Katie and Andrew for their help with this book. My special thanks to Marjorie Stadnycki and Jodi Wing for their talents and dedication.

Lastly I am grateful to Cedco Publishing for believing in my visions and making this book a reality.

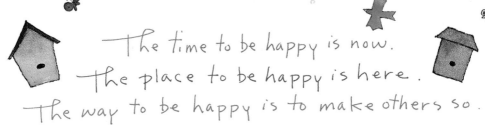

The time to be happy is now.
The place to be happy is here.
The way to be happy is to make others so.

. Robert Ingersoll · 1883-1899

Although the message is timeless, what better opportunity than the dawning of a new millennium to fully awaken to the possibilities of the "here and now"! We all need a gentle reminder from time to time to live fully in the present. Stress can easily get the better of us in this fast-paced world. It's all we can do to keep pace with the demands on our time and energy, let alone to remember that there are many simple pleasures awaiting us ... a wondrous sunrise to behold each morning, the child who's waiting for a hug, or that much needed moment of solitude with a warm cup of tea that is ours for the taking. Life is full of precious moments, but we must not only be open to them ... we must invite them ... we must make them happen.

We all deserve a life that is rich with beauty, meaning, laughter and love

All too often we find ourselves saying "Someday..." or "Things will be different when..." The arrival of the new millennium marks a milestone for our place in history and serves to remind us how quickly time passes.

Don't let the magic of the moment pass you by.

Celebrate the simple pleasures ☕

🌸 Awaken to nature's beauty

Rejoice in small miracles 🦋

☺ Smile at a stranger

Hug the one you love ♡

❀ Be good to yourself ◎

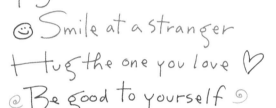

Build your bridge 🎵 Sing your song ♫ Make your mark ✏

Don't forget to fly

🌸

Stop waiting for Tomorrow

The time to be happy
is
now.

All My Best! ♡ Kathy

Whatever you do,

or dream you can,

BEGIN it.

. Goethe .
1749 - 1832

Each Day is a Gift • Each Day is a Gift • Each Day is a Gift • Each Day is a Gift

• Make the Most of it! •

May you Live
all the days
of your life

Jonathan
Swift
1667-1745

Rich as he is,
not even the emperor
can buy back
one single day

.Chinese proverb.

That man is richest
whose pleasures are cheapest.

.Henry David Thoreau.
1817 - 1862

Rich are they
who treasure
simple
joys.

The past is history.
The future a mystery.
But today is a gift
which is why
it is called
the

present

·unknown·

To me, every hour of the day and night is an unspeakable, perfect
MIRACLE

·WALT WHITMAN·
1819-1892

WRITE IT ON YOUR

Heart ♥

that everyday

is the BEST DAY of the

Year.

·EMERSON·

The best way to secure
future happiness
is to be
as happy
as is rightfully possible

today

· Charles W. Eliot ·
1834 - 1926

 Life is ours to be spent, not to be saved.

·DH Lawrence·
1895 - 1930

How
beautiful a Day can be
when
Kindness
touches it.

G. Elliston

All who *joy* would win
must share it.
Happiness
was born a twin.

· Lord Byron ·
1788 - 1824

The best portion of a good man's life
is his little, nameless, unremembered
acts of kindness and love.

William
· Wordsworth ·
1770 - 1850

Happiness is the result
of making
a
Bouquet

of those flowers
within reach.

·Proverb·

I am still determined to be cheerful and happy in whatever situation I may be, for I have also learned from experience that the greater part of our happiness or misery depends on our dispositions and not our circumstances.

·Martha Washington·
1732-1802

Imitate the Sundial's ways

Count only the pleasant days

· German Proverb ·

The really happy man
is the one who can
enjoy the scenery
when he has to take
a

Détour

Happiness is not a state to
arrive at,
but rather a manner
of traveling.

.Samuel Johnson.
1709 - 1784

Those who bring SUNSHINE to the lives of others cannot keep it from themselves.

·James Barrie.

... The way to be *happy* is to make others so.

. Robert Ingersoll.

Live in each Season as it passes

breathe the air, drink the drink, taste the fruit.

Henry David Thoreau.
1817-1862

A little garden
in which to walk,
an immensity in which to
dream.
at one's feet that which can
be cultivated and plucked;
overhead that which one can
study and meditate upon;
some herbs on earth
and all the
stars in the sky

· Hugo ·

Heaven

is under
our feet
as well as over our heads.

·Henry David Thoreau·
1817 - 1862

Give me books, fruit, French wine
and fine weather and a little music
out of doors,
played by someone I do not know.

·John Keats·
1795 - 1821

Happiness

is a habit

Cultivate it

Elbert
Hubbard
1856-1915

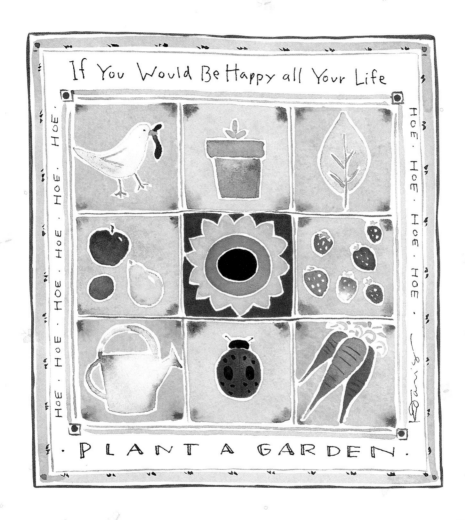

There is
always
Music
amongst the trees
in the garden

... but our hearts must be
very quiet to hear it.

Learn to be

Silent

Let your quiet mind listen and absorb.

.Pythagoras.
582 - 500 B.C.

There is a pleasure in the pathless woods.

.Lord Byron.
1788 - 1824

A bird
does not sing
because it has
an answer,
it sings because
it has
a
SoNG

·proverb·

The most evident token
and apparent sign of
true wisdom
is a
constant and unconstrained

rejoicing

· Michael de Montaigne ·
1533 - 1592

If you keep within your heart a green bough,
there will come one day, to stay,
a singing bird.

· Arabian Proverb.

alas
for those
who never sing
but die with all their
music in them.

· Oliver Wendell Holmes ·
1809 - 1894

I have spent my days stringing and unstringing
my instrument
while the song I came to sing remains unsung.

· Rabindranath Tagore ·
1861 - 1941

Twenty years from now you will be more disappointed by
the things you didn't do than by the ones you did.
So, throw off the bowlines, sail away from the safe
harbor, catch the trade winds in your sails.
Explore · Dream

· Mark Twain ·   1835 - 1910

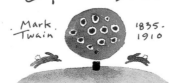

To See the
World
in a grain of sand,
and heaven in a wildflower,
hold infinity in the palm of your hand,
& eternity in an hour.

·William Blake·
1757-1827

MAY YOUR LIFE BE LIKE A
WILDFLOWER
GROWING FREELY IN THE
BEAUTY & JOY OF EACH DAY
· INDIAN PROVERB ·

Why Not TODAY

Mend a quarre[l]
Write a l[etter]
treasure
Encourage
Find the T[ime]
Listen • Apol[ogize]
Think first of someone else
Laugh a little
gratitude • Laugh
Gladden
pleasure in the beau[ty]
of the earth
love
Speak it still

Seek out a forgotten friend
letter • Share some
e a soft answer •
th •keep a promise•
•Forgive an enemy
e if you were wrong
e kind and gentle •
ittle more • Express your
heart of a child • Take
and wonder
eak your
eak it again•
e again •

Everyone should carefully observe
which way his heart
draws him,
and then choose that way
with all his
strengths.

· Hasidic saying ·

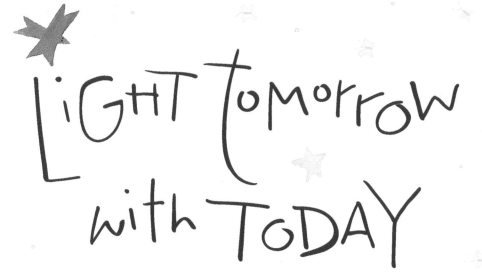

LiGHT Tomorrow with TODAY

· Elizabeth Barrett Browning ·
1806 - 1861

Never put off until tomorrow
what you can do today,
because if you enjoy it today,
you can do it again
tomorrow.

· Anonymous ·

One joy scatters
a hundred griefs.
-Chinese Proverb.

Time spent laughing
is time spent with the
·Japanese Proverb.

Joy is a net of love
by which you can catch souls.
·Mother Teresa.
1910.
1997

Unshared joy
is an unlighted candle.
·Spanish Proverb.

If you tickle yourself, you can laugh when you like
.Chinese Proverb.

Scatter joy

Ralph Waldo Emerson
1803· 1882

And we should consider every day lost on which we have not danced at least once.
·Friedrich Nietzche· 1844·1900

You never really
leave a place
you love.

Part of it
you take with you
leaving
a part of you
behind.

Those who are happiest,
whether king or peasant,
are those
who find peace
in their

HOME

A small home
holds
as much
happiness
as a big one.

·proverb·

Very little is needed to make
a happy life.
It is all within

yourself,

in your way
of
thinking.

·Marcus Aurelius·
121-180

Our greatest danger in life is in permitting the
urgent things to crowd out the important.

·Oliver Wendell Holmes·
1809-1894

MAY THE SUN shine
upon You
May LOVE SURROUND
You
May the LIGHT WITHIN
You
Guide You always

Hold out your hands
to feel the
luxury of
Sunbeams.

·unknown·

Remember the moments of the past, Look forward to the promise of the future,

But
most of all,
Celebrate
the
present,
for it is
precious.

Kathy Davis has always loved art. A former teacher, she designed her new career as an artist and writer one greeting card at a time. Her colorful style and uplifting messages now adorn thousands of products found worldwide. A favorite quote of hers, "The sky's the limit when your heart's in it," speaks to her success. A bluebird in flight, one of Kathy's signature images, helps to illustrate her newfound creative freedom. Kathy loves nature, and many of her designs reflect her favorite subjects of sunshine, flowers and animals. Inspiration and humor often find their way into the original verse and quotations that adorn her creations. Kathy lives in the Philadelphia area with her family and a menagerie of pets.